Copyright © 2021 by Jack smith

All rights reserved. No part of this publication may be reproduced, distributed, or transmitted in any form or by any means, including photocopying, recording, or other electronic or mechanical methods, without the prior written permission of the publisher, except in the case of brief quotations embodied in critical reviews and certain other noncommercial uses permitted by copyright law.

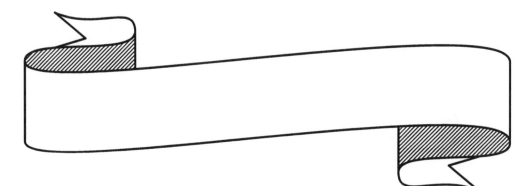

this book belongs to :

_____

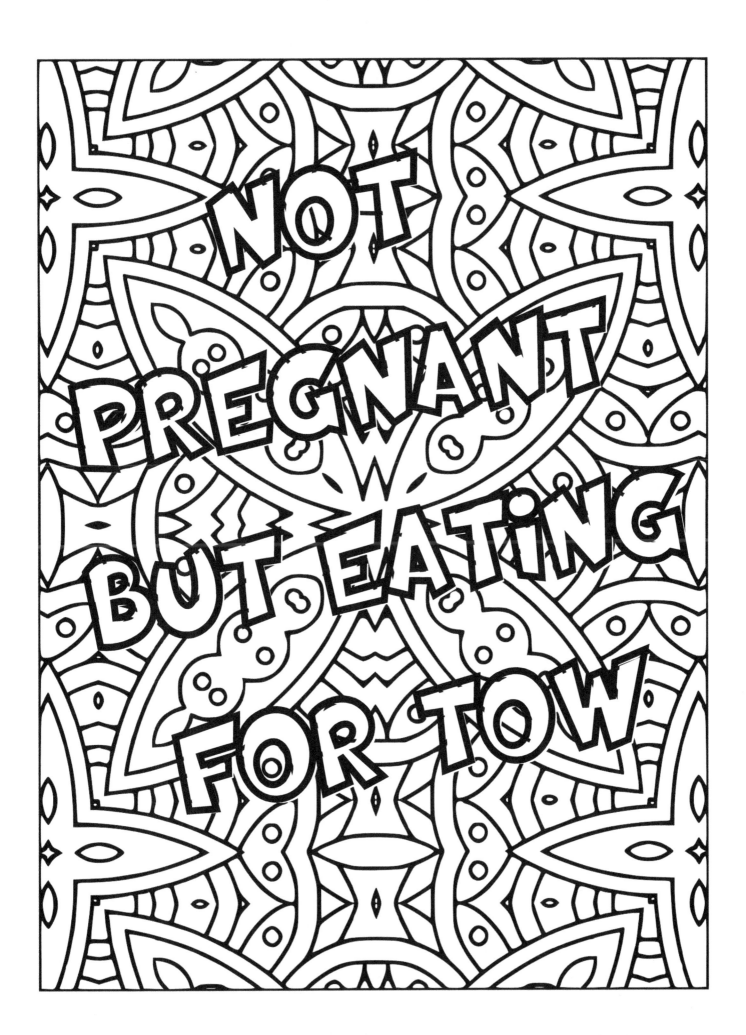

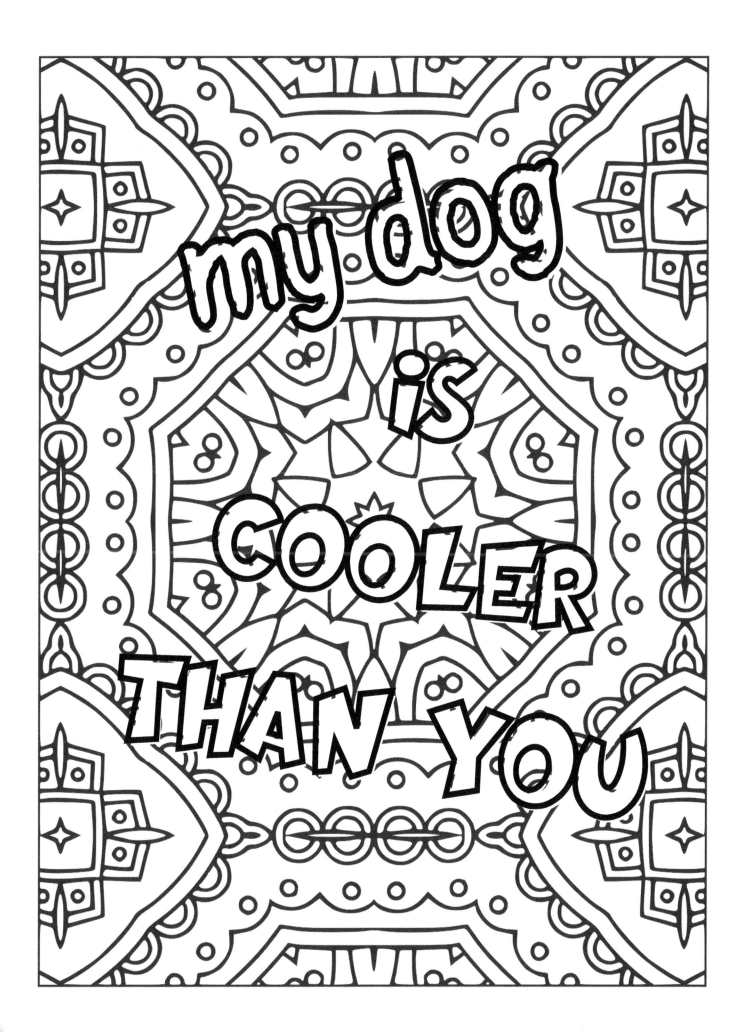

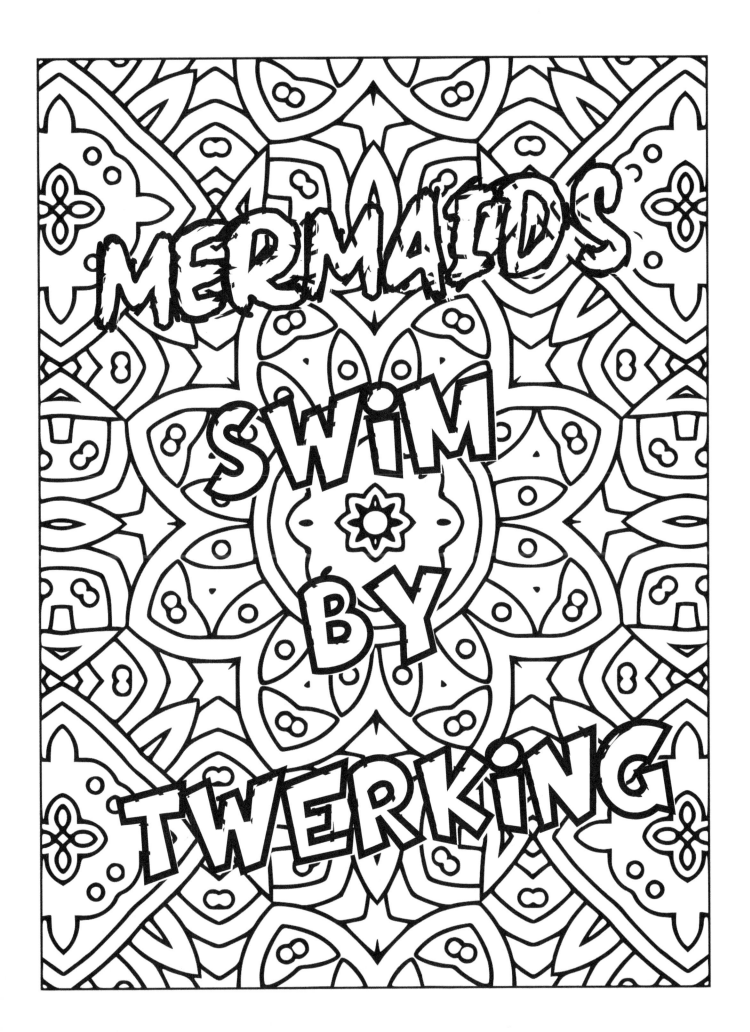

LIVE FOOTLOOSE & NOTHING

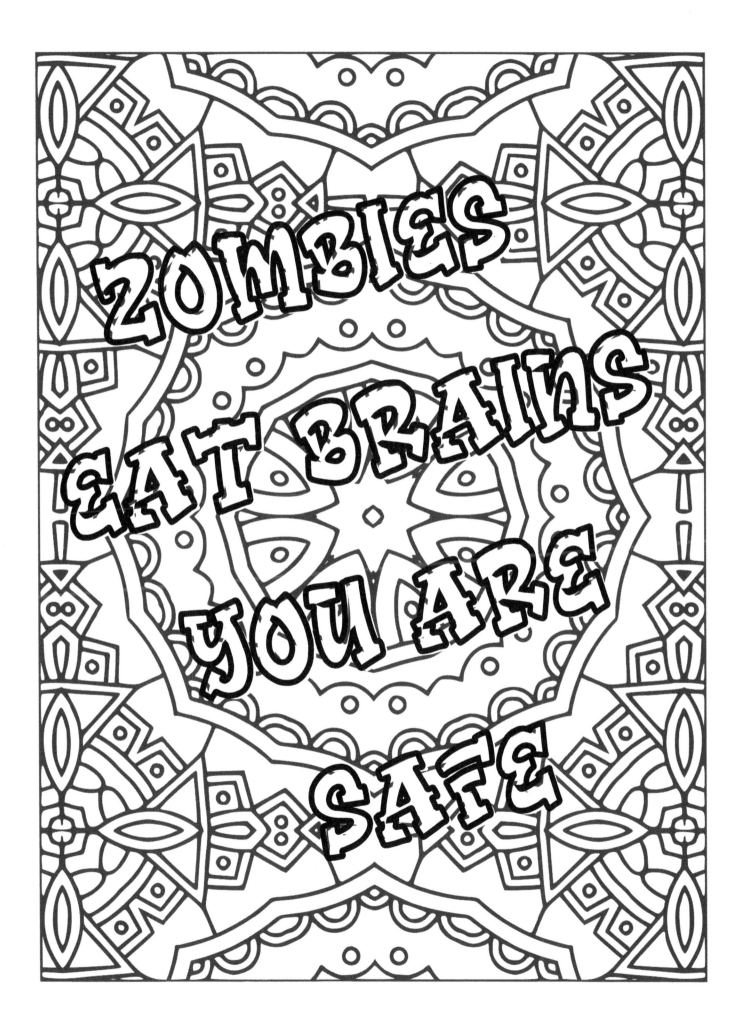

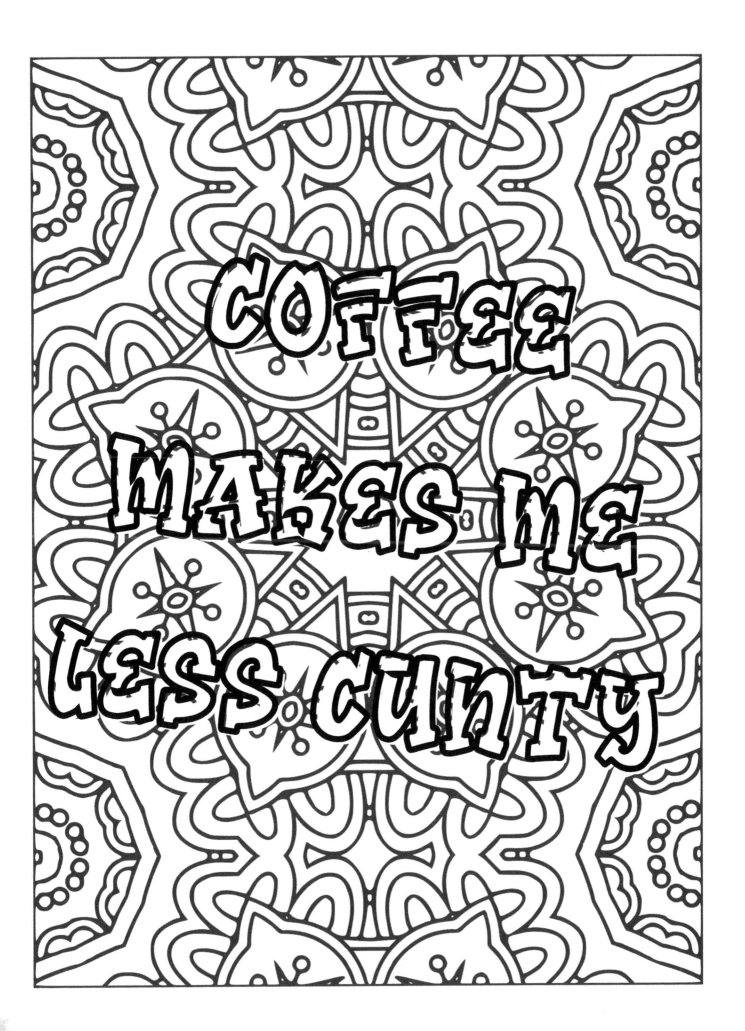

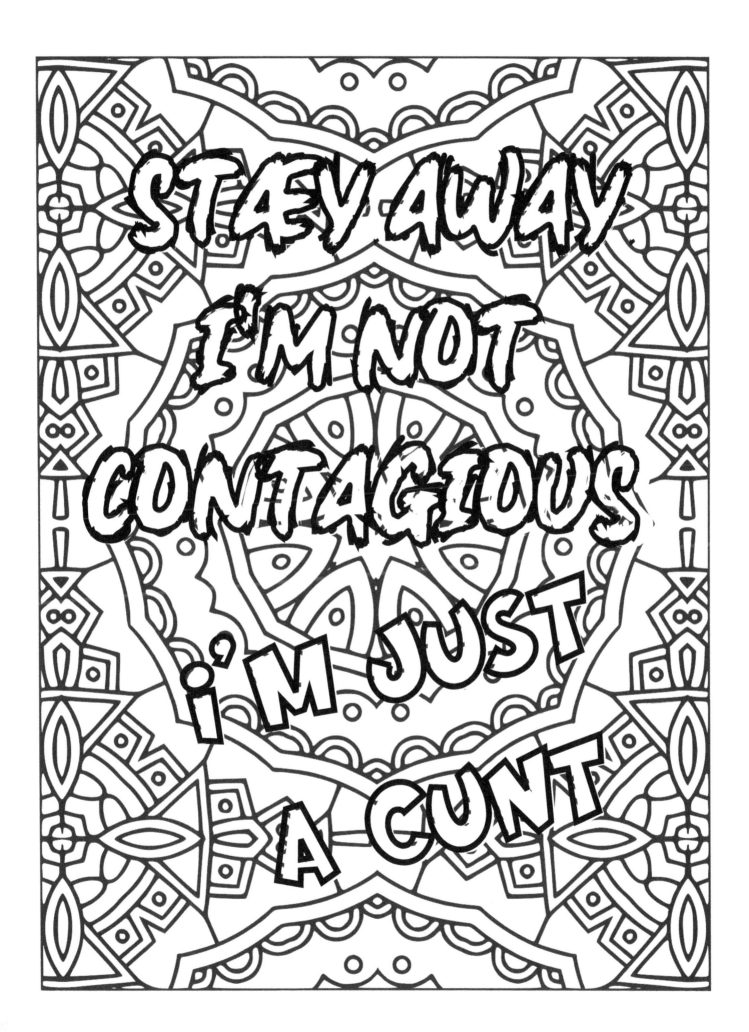

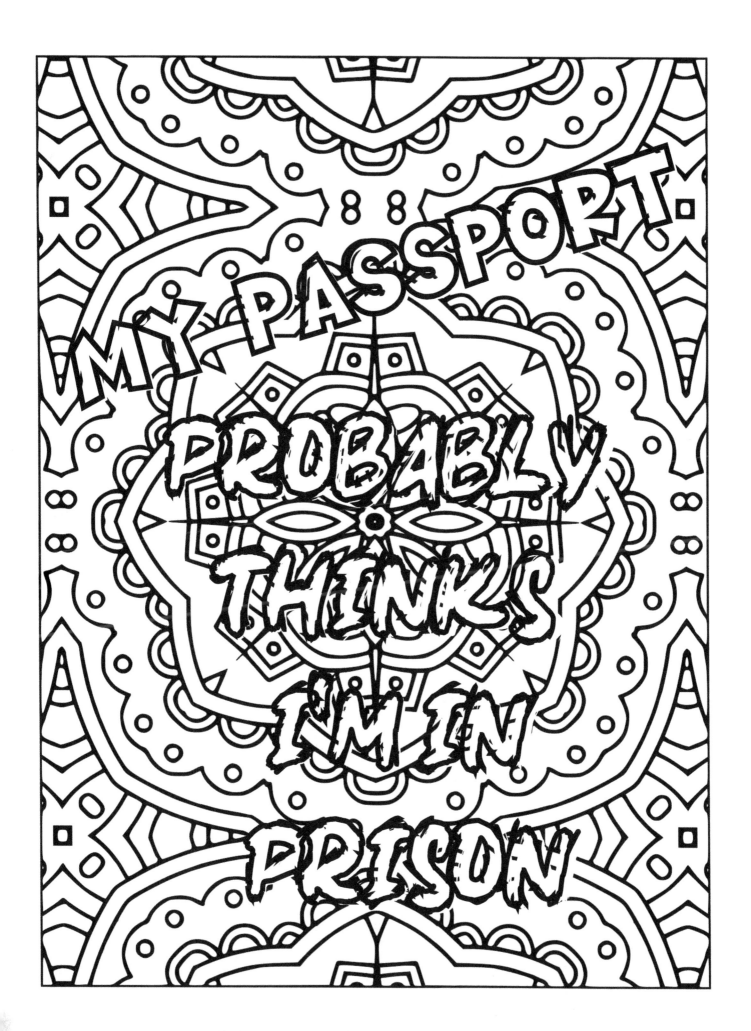

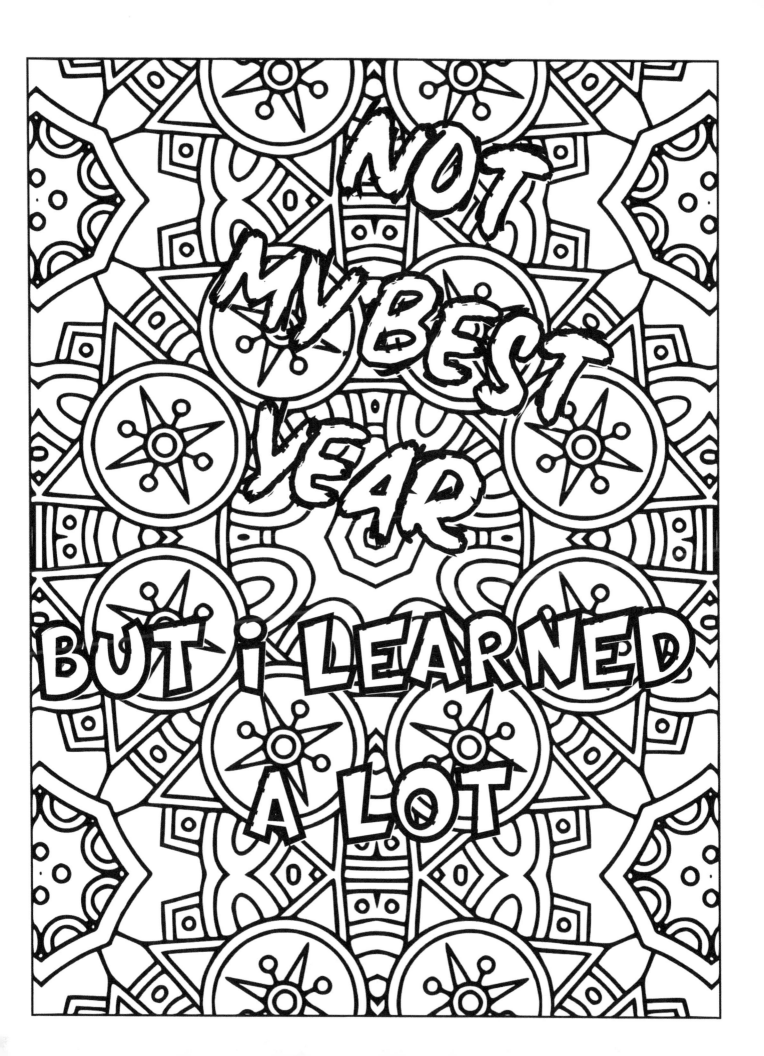

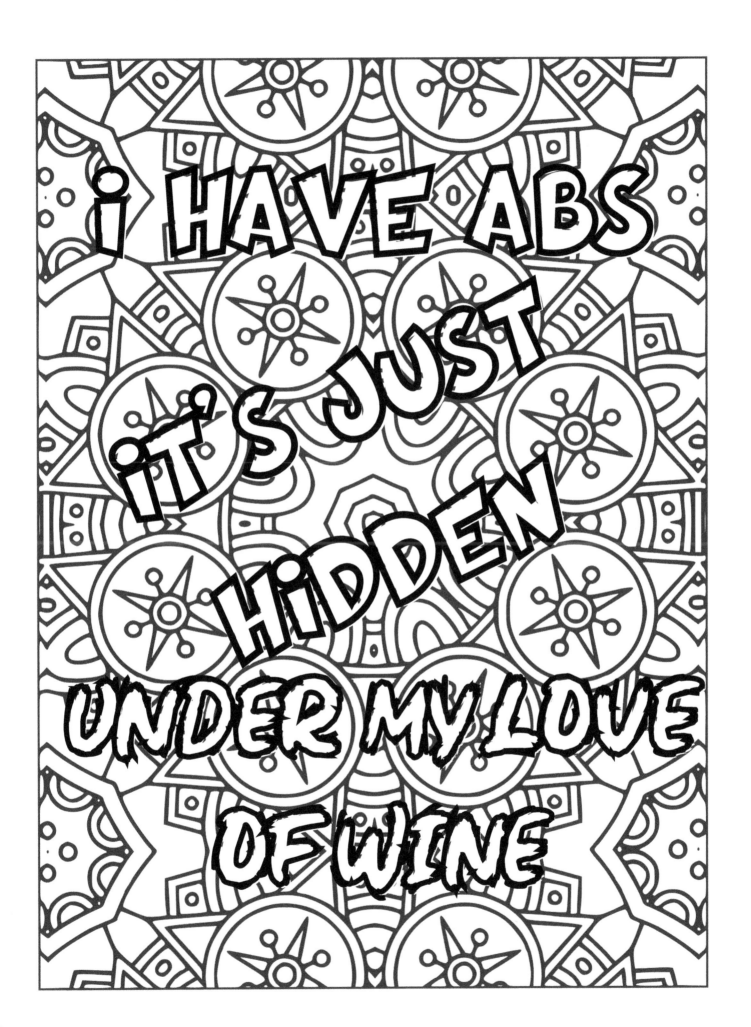

Printed in the USA
CPSIA information can be obtained
at www.ICGtesting.com
LVHW081603041224
798324LV00015B/1536